D0297500

00 401 056 754

CELEBRITY SECRETS

FASHION MODELS

ADAM SUTHERLAND

WAYLAND

First published in 2012 by Wayland

Wayland
338 Euston Road
London NW1 3BH

Wayland Australia
Level 17/207 Kent Street
Sydney, NSW 2000

Editor: Nicola Edwards
Designer: Emil Dacanay
Picture Researcher: Shelley Noronha

Picture Acknowledgements: The author and publisher would like to thank the following for allowing their pictures to be reproduced in this publication:

Cover: Lev Radin / Shutterstock.com; title page: Cinemafestival/Shutterstock.com; p2 Lev Radin / Shutterstock.com; p4 Helga Esteb / Shutterstock.com; p5 360b / Shutterstock.com; p6 Featureflash / Shutterstock.com; p7 Dave M. Benett/Getty Images; p8 cinemafestival / Shutterstock.com; p9 C.J. LaFrance/ Istock; p10 Lev Radin / Shutterstock. com; p11 Vallery Jean/FilmMagic/ Getty Images; p12 Marc Piasecki/WireImage/ Getty Images; p13 Edouard BERNAUX/ Gamma-Rapho via Getty Images; p14 Gareth Cattermole/Getty Images; p15 Jacopo Raule/Getty Images; p16 Helga Esteb / Shutterstock.com; p17 Andrew H. Walker/ Getty Images for Get Schooled; p18 Michael N. Todaro/FilmMagic/Getty Images; p19 Mike Coppola/FilmMagic/Getty Images; p20 Mike Coppola/Getty Images for IMG; p21 Pierre Verdy/AFP/Getty Images; p22 (t) Helga Esteb / Shutterstock.com, (m) Natalia Yeromina / Shutterstock.com. (b) Valerie Macon/Getty Images; p23 (t) Eduardo Parra/WireImage/Getty Images, (m) Bryan Bedder/Getty Images, (b) John Parra/Getty Images for Victoria's Secret; p24 © Kletr/ Shutterstock.com

British Library Cataloguing in Publication Data

Sutherland, Adam.
Fashion models. – (Celebrity secrets)
1. Models (Persons)–Biography–Juvenile literature.
I. Title II. Series
746.9'2'0922-dc23

ISBN: 978 0 7502 6775 5

Printed in China

Wayland is a division of Hachette Children's Books, an Hachette UK company

www.hachette.co.uk

Contents

Gisele Bündchen

TOP-EARNING SUPERMODEL

Gisele is the most successful and highest paid model in the world, with an estimated income in 2011 of US$45 million (£29 million).

Stats!

Full name: Gisele Caroline Bündchen

Date and place of birth: 20 July 1980 in Três de Maio, Rio Grande do Sul, Brazil

Stats: Height 5ft 11in (1.80m), dress size 6 UK

First break: At 14, Gisele was spotted in São Paulo by a model scout, and was entered into the national Elite Look of the Year contest where she came second. She then travelled to Ibiza for the World Look of the Year contest and finished fourth.

Major achievements: Gisele has worked with some of the biggest names in fashion – Dolce & Gabbana, Chloé, Dior, Ralph Lauren, Versace and many more. She has appeared on over 600 magazine covers, and has successfully launched her own range of sandals and beauty products.

Secrets of success: Gisele's wholesome sun-kissed looks arrived at the perfect time in the fashion industry. Clients and photographers say she is as hard-working as she is beautiful.

Gisele has five sisters. Her twin, Patrícia, is her manager. Gabriela is her lawyer, Raquel is her accountant and Rafaela works on Gisele's website. Her other sister Graziela is a judge!

Life Story

At school, Gisele was so tall and skinny that classmates nicknamed her 'Olive Oyl' after cartoon character Popeye's beanpole girlfriend. Nevertheless, her mother enrolled 13-year-old Gisele and two of her sisters on a modelling course, which ended with a trip to São Paulo – a 29-hour drive from Gisele's home town. While in the city, Gisele was spotted by a scout from model agency Elite.

In 1996 Gisele made her catwalk debut at New York Fashion Week, followed by London Fashion Week in 1997 where she made her mark at the Alexander McQueen show. By 2000, she had signed a record-breaking US$25m (£16m) contract with lingerie brand Victoria's Secret and became the most successful and highest-paid model of the decade.

Gisele smiles for the cameras at the launch of her new shoe collection, Ipanema Gisele Bündchen, in Berlin in 2008.

Questions and Answers

Q What made you decide to move away from home at 14 to be a model?

A 'I didn't want to leave my family, but my parents were working and I had five sisters, so things were [tough]. I figured I could be independent and work. I thought I could take care of myself and it would be one less child for them to worry about.'

Gisele Bündchen, *Harper's Bazaar* 2009

Q How do you react to people criticising your look?

A 'When I started modelling, some people were like "She's never going to make it!" But not everybody has to like me. Some people like watermelon; some people like pineapple. It doesn't mean that watermelon is better. People have different tastes.'

Gisele Bündchen, *Vanity Fair* 2009

Gisele's face on a website or billboard causes sales to soar, and her own sandal brand, Ipanema Gisele Bündchen is now a worldwide success, selling 250 million pairs in 2010 alone. She donates a portion of the profits to saving the Amazon rainforest, and also works for the UN Environment Programme as a Goodwill Ambassador. The caring, sharing supermodel!

Kate Moss

BEST OF BRITISH

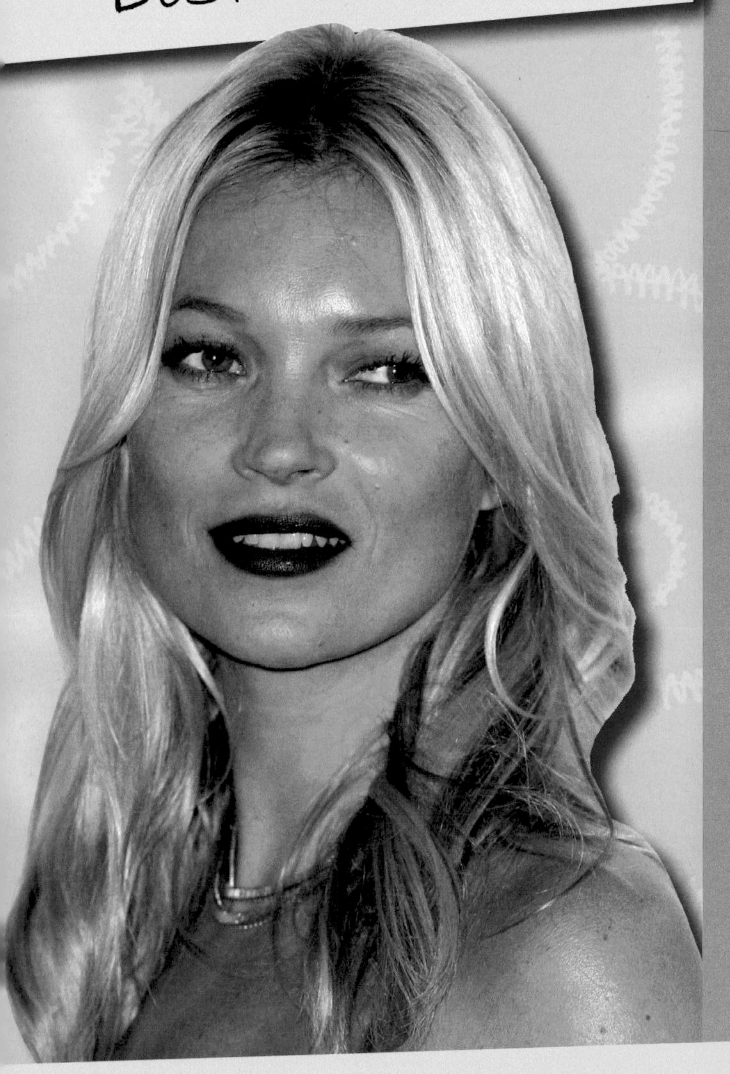

Kate arriving for a Rimmel party in London in 2011. She has been a face of the brand since 2005.

Stats!

Full name: Kate Moss

Date and place of birth: 16 January 1974 in Addiscombe, Croydon, UK

Stats: Height 5ft 7in (1.70m), dress size 6 UK

First break: At 14 years old, Kate was spotted at JFK Airport in New York by Sarah Doukas, the founder of Storm Models. She did her first catwalk – for designer John Galliano – aged 15. At 16, a black and white shoot with photographer Corinne Day for fashion magazine *The Face* brought Kate to the attention of the fashion world.

Major achievements: Kate is probably Britain's most successful model. She has appeared on the cover of *British Vogue* 30 times, and has been the face of Rimmel London since 2005. She has fronted campaigns for Gucci, Dolce & Gabbana, Calvin Klein, Chanel, Burberry and many others.

Secrets of success: Although relatively short for a fashion model, Kate's young, fresh-faced look and lack of curves – the 'waif' look – proved a popular contrast to established big names like Cindy Crawford and Claudia Schiffer.

In 2005, a painting of Kate by the late artist Lucian Freud sold at auction for £3.93 million.

Life Story

Kate Moss's parents split up when she was just 14. To help her get over the upset and upheaval, Kate's dad took her on holiday to the Bahamas. On the way back to England they changed planes in New York and bumped into Sarah Doukas, the model agent who would change Kate's life.

Kate wasn't an overnight success. She remembers walking the streets of London, attending 7-8 castings per day for close to four years before she started to get some breaks. At 18, she appeared in ads for Calvin Klein fragrance CK One. By 20, she was dating film star Johnny Depp, and flying backwards and forwards from New York to London up to eight times per week!

Kate at the launch of her Topshop collection in November 2010. Her designs often sell out in hours!

Questions and Answers

Q Do you still enjoy modelling?

A '[I love it!] Somebody said the other day, most models don't like fashion, they just do it as a job. I was horrified. My God, why would you do it? If you don't enjoy it... if you don't get into the spirit, what's the point?

Kate Moss, *The Telegraph* 2009

Q Why do you think your Topshop range has been so successful?

A 'I don't think people buy these things because they want to look like me. They buy them because they know I [understand] about fashion, about fit. And so I should. I've had 20 years of clothes on my back.'

Kate Moss, *The Observer* 2009

Although she still models regularly, Kate has also been designing her own range of clothes for Topshop since 2007 – a deal that reportedly earns her £1m per year, and brings in £40m in annual sales. Kate's great fashion sense means she is rarely out of the UK press, and now fans can buy some of that Kate Moss cool for themselves!

Lily Cole

ENGLISH ROSE

Model turned actress: Lily at the Cannes Film Festival in 2009, attending the screening of her film 'The Imaginarium Of Doctor Parnassus'.

Stats!

Full name: Lily Luahana Cole

Date and place of birth: 19 May 1988 in Torquay, UK

Stats: Height 5ft 10in (1.79m), dress size 6 UK

First break: At 14 years old, Lily was spotted in Covent Garden in London by a scout from Storm Models. By 15, she was on the catwalk for designers such as Alexander McQueen and John Galliano, and working with Madonna's favourite photographer Steven Meisel. At 16 she was on the cover of Vogue and named Model of the Year at the British Fashion Awards.

Major achievements: Lily has a contract with cosmetics brand Rimmel London. She has also worked with Chanel, Hermes, Prada, Moschino and high street giant Marks and Spencer. Outside modelling, Lily also has a degree in history of art from Cambridge University.

Secrets of success: Lily's extraordinary looks – flame red hair, porcelain doll features, and long legs – have helped her stand out from the crowd.

In 2010, Lily appeared as a 'sea siren' in an episode of Dr Who, which was filmed while she was studying for her final exams at Cambridge.

Life Story

Lily Cole mixes beauty with brains. She has a double first from Cambridge, where she studied history of art. Juggling a model's hectic schedule with the demands of student life, she used to read textbooks in the hair and make-up chair, and caught up on university essays during transatlantic flights between modelling assignments.

Lily on the red carpet at the Toronto International Film Festival 2009.

A model since she was 14, Lily quickly rose through the ranks, working with a who's who of great fashion brands and appearing on magazine covers from the US to Japan and everywhere in between. On the runway, she has modelled for Chanel, Versace, Jasper Conran and Louis Vuitton. In 2009, she was named by *French Vogue* as one of the top 30 models of the decade.

Most recently, Lily has moved into acting, making a guest appearance in the 2007 film *St Trinian's*. She has since worked alongside Johnny Depp and the late Heath Ledger in *The Imaginarium of Doctor Parnassus*. Is there no end to her talents?

Questions and Answers

Q Has being a model made you more confident about your looks?

A 'I definitely never thought of myself as model material. Me on a catwalk with all those superwomen? [Success] has given me a lot of self confidence, but I wouldn't say I feel beautiful. On the other hand, I don't feel ugly!'

Lily Cole, *Welt Online* 2010

Q Did you ever wish you weren't a redhead?

A 'I used to be teased [at school] for having red hair and that made me very insecure. Now I love it! I only think I look unusual now because lots of people have told me so.'

Lily Cole, *The Times* 2009

Tyson Beckford

THE FIRST MALE SUPERMODEL

Tyson's exotic good looks and athletic physique helped him become the best known male model in the world.

Tyson has appeared in music videos for 50 Cent, Britney Spears and the Pet Shop Boys!

Stats!

Full name: Tyson Craig Beckford

Date and place of birth: 19 December 1970 in The Bronx, New York, USA

Stats: Height 5ft 10in (182cm), chest 40in (101cm), waist 30in (76cm)

First break: In 1991, Tyson was spotted playing American football in the park by a writer for music magazine *The Source*, who asked him to model for their fashion pages. From there, Tyson found himself an agent and started shooting his first big jobs for the *New York Times*, *GQ* and the Marks and Spencer catalogue.

Major achievements: In 1993 Tyson was chosen by fashion designer Ralph Lauren to be the face of his Polo line of sportswear. He was the first black male model to feature in the company's advertising. The first campaign was a huge success and Tyson quickly signed a two-year deal with the brand. He also appeared in Gucci and Calvin Klein ad campaigns, becoming the world's first male supermodel!

Secrets of success: Tyson's striking good looks are a mixture of his Jamaican and Chinese roots. According to Ralph Lauren, Tyson has 'an all-American look with a dramatic edge'.

Life Story

Tyson got a taste of modelling at a very early age. His mother was a part-time fashion model, who often took her young son along on castings, or to sit backstage when she had fashion shows. Even so, the young man never thought he was cut out for the profession, and spent his time on the American football field rather than the fashion catwalk.

However, his mother also passed on the exotic looks that would lead her son to fame and fortune. Discovered in a New York park, Tyson quickly rose to the top of the modelling profession. He won a series of awards, including VH1's Man of the Year, and paved the way for models of colour – both men and women.

Tyson and actress Calandra Glenn performing in the play 'Loving Him Is Killing Me' in Miami, Florida in 2011.

Questions and Answers

Q You spent the first seven years of your life in Jamaica. What was it like moving to New York?

A 'A total culture shock. All the kids spoke perfect English, and I had picked up this Jamaican [dialect] so I was sent to English classes to get rid of it. Plus I had never even seen snow before!'

Tyson Beckford, *emcBlue* 2011

Q Why did you move from modelling to acting?

A 'Modelling's been [great], but my heart has always been in acting. When I was discovered in New York I was picking up the paper looking for acting jobs. I wasn't looking for modelling jobs because I didn't think I was model material.'

Tyson Beckford, *emcBlue* 2011

Today, Tyson has swapped the still camera for the moving camera, and returned to his first love – acting. He has starred in, and produced, a number of films including the modelling comedy *Zoolander* (2001), *Hotel California* (2008) and *Dream Street* (2010).

Baptiste Giabiconi

THE FABULOUS FRENCHMAN

Baptiste strikes a pose at the Chanel autumn/winter 2011/2012 show as part of Paris Fashion Week in 2011.

Stats!

Full name: Baptiste Giabiconi

Date and place of birth: 8 November 1989 in Marignane, France

Stats: Height 6ft 2in (1.88m), chest 40in (101cm), waist 31in (79cm)

First break: Baptiste moved to Paris from the south of France when he was 18 to start modelling. He was spotted in a fashion magazine by the legendary designer and photographer Karl Lagerfeld, who called in Baptiste for a test shoot. Lagerfeld was so impressed he made Bapiste the male face of his label Chanel.

Major achievements: Baptiste is currently the face of Fendi and Karl Lagerfeld as well as Chanel, and has worked with Roberto Cavali, Giorgio Armani, and fashion magazines *Vogue, Harper's Bazaar* and more. He was also listed Number 1 in the top 50 international male models on website www.models.com for an amazing two years.

Secrets of success: Karl Lagerfeld describes Baptiste as 'a boy version of Gisele – skinny, but with an athletic body – [perfect] for clothes.'

Before he became a model Baptiste worked in a factory building helicopters.

Life Story

When he was growing up in Marseilles, on the French Mediterranean coast, all Baptiste wanted to do was run his own pizza-delivery business. He had left school at 14 to train in the hotel and catering industry, and by 17 was working several part-time jobs to save money towards his dream.

Questions and Answers

Q What did you family think when you left home for Paris?

A 'My mother was so nervous for me... but she thinks everything that has happened in the past two years is amazing. The first thing I bought with my first big paycheck was a piece of jewellery for [her].'

Baptiste Giabiconi, *This is London* 2011

Q Did you imagine that meeting Karl Lagerfeld would be so life-changing?

A 'Honestly, I just wanted to learn as much as I could. I saw it as an amazing experience and [at the very least] I would get some great photos for my book.'

Baptiste Giabiconi, *This is London* 2011

Baptiste performs at the opening of a Young Designers fashion show in May 2011.

Baptiste was self-conscious about his skinny frame, and had started going to the gym to try to develop some muscles. A fellow gym member saw his potential and suggested he have some pictures taken and try to get signed to a model agency. Twelve months later Baptiste was in Paris, and one of the hottest new models in town!

Baptiste has always been a big music fan and has already released a debut single 'Showtime'. He plans to follow it up with an album but has no plans to give up modelling just yet. The first singing, dancing model? We wouldn't bet against it!

David Gandy

THE MAN OF THE MOMENT

The name's Gandy, David Gandy: the British model strikes a James Bond pose at a Dolce & Gabbana party in London in July 2011.

David has a degree in marketing from the University of Gloucestershire.

Stats!

Full name: David James Gandy

Date and place of birth: 19 February 1980 in Billericay, Essex, UK

Stats: Height 6ft 2in (1.88m), chest 41in (104cm), waist 34.5in (87cm)

First break: A friend entered David for a model search run by daytime TV show *Richard and Judy.* At first judges put his name on the 'no' pile but then changed their minds. He went on to win the competition and was given a contract with Select model agency.

Major achievements: In 2006 David shot with world famous photographer Mario Testino for the Dolce & Gabbana fragrance 'Light Blue Pour Homme'. The shoot helped David become the best-known and highest-paid male model in the world! Since then, he has worked regularly for Dolce & Gabbana, and for other fashion brands including Stefanel.

Secrets of success: David's strong and muscular look changed the face of male fashion. Before him, designers were using teenage boys for ultra-skinny suits. David reintroduced muscles to men's fashion!

Life Story

David Gandy had to wait five years to become an overnight success. He won a modelling competition in 2001 and started working regularly for menswear catalogues and high street brands. He was flying backwards and forwards across the Atlantic 60-70 times per year on modelling assignments. But he wasn't happy. So he told his model agency to cancel all the catalogue work and push for big-name fashion labels. David's persistence paid off.

David arrives in style at a Dolce & Gabbana event during Milan Fashion Week in June 2011.

Dolce & Gabbana flew him to Los Angeles to shoot with photographer Steven Meisel, then rebooked him for the Light Blue fragrance launch. Before he knew it, David's picture was on 50-foot billboards in New York's Times Square!

Questions and Answers

Q What did you think when you saw the Light Blue billboard?

A '[I never actually saw it!] Some friends of mine were in New York and sent me pictures... If I had seen it I'm not sure how I would have felt. Probably nothing, to be honest. It's a persona. It's not really me.'

David Gandy, The Telegraph 2010

Q Did that ad change your life?

A '[Completely.] Before then I would turn up for castings to find 500 hopefuls already there, [and] get ordered to wear a T-shirt that 300 sweaty guys had already worn!'

David Gandy, *The Times* 2009

At school, David was teased for his lack of fashion sense. Now he is one of the most in-demand male models in the world. His muscular, masculine look has changed male fashion and he is now trying to help British men dress better with a menswear blog for Vogue.com and a style guide app for the iPhone. David seems to achieve everything he puts his mind to.

Tyra Banks

TV SUPERSTAR

Beauty and brains: Tyra has made the move from successful model to successful TV producer.

America's Next Top Model is shown in over 170 countries and earns Tyra an estimated US$18m (£11m) per year!

Stats!

Full name: Tyra Lynne Banks

Date and place of birth: 4 December 1973 in Inglewood, California, USA
Stats: Height 5ft 10in (1.79m), dress size 10 UK

First break: Tyra started modelling at high school as a hobby. She intended to go to university to study film, but through her model agency she was introduced to a French scout who invited her over to Europe. In Paris she was offered 25 catwalk shows, including Chanel, Karl Lagerfeld and Yves Saint Laurent. She put the education on hold, and became a full-time model.

Major achievements: During her modelling career, Tyra was the first African-American woman on the covers of *GQ* and *Sports Illustrated*'s annual swimsuit issue. She was also the first African-American on the cover of the Victoria's Secret catalogue. Now retired from modelling, she owns a television production company, Bankable Productions, which makes *America's Next Top Model*.

Secrets of success: Tyra always focused on the next step in her career. She started out in fashion, but realised she could be more successful as a commercial model so pursued that. Then, as she grew older, she made the move into TV presenting and producing.

Life Story

When 17-year-old Tyra Banks was invited to Paris to meet the famous French fashion houses, she knew virtually nothing about fashion, and very little about modelling. So she borrowed books and fashion magazines from the local library, and watched catwalk clips on TV. She even practised walking around wearing her mum's longest dress and highest heels.

Tyra takes to the stage for a Get Schooled Foundation visit to a New York school in October 2011.

The homework paid off, and Tyra was an instant hit in Paris. Her mum became her manager and the pair carefully steered Tyra's career from fashion to successful commercial contracts with high street brands Nike, McDonald's and Covergirl, and then into film and television.

Questions and Answers

Q As an African-American model, did you meet a lot of obstacles?

A 'Every single day of my modelling career, I encountered prejudice. They'd say 'You can't be on this cover.' 'You can't do this campaign.' It never made me bitter, but it did make me hungrier to prove [people] wrong.'

Tyra Banks, *The New York Times* 2008

Q How easy was it to switch from modelling into TV?

A 'When I went into producing, my biggest obstacle was that I was a model. But anybody who is at the top of anything has taken risks and withstood criticism... I say: 'You think I'm just a model? Well, then, let me show you'!'

Tyra Banks, *The New York Times* 2008

Tyra retired from modelling in 2005 with a final appearance on the catwalk for lingerie brand Victoria's Secret. Since then she has presented her own talk show, *The Tyra Banks Show*, created and produced *America's Next Top Model*, and is even writing a series of fictional books on modelling called *Modelland*.

Crystal Renn

THE PLUS-SIZE SUPERSTAR

Picture perfect: Crystal lost 30 kg (60 lb) to become a fashion model, but found real success when she reverted to her naturally curvy figure.

Stats!

Full name: Crystal Renn

Date and place of birth: 18 June 1986 in Miami, Florida USA

Stats: Height 5ft 9in (1.75m), dress size 12-14 UK

First break: Crystal was discovered by a model scout at 14 and told she could be the next Gisele Bündchen if she lost 23cm (9 inches) off her hips. A year later, she had lost the weight, and moved to New York to become a fashion model. But constant dieting and exercise were damaging Crystal's health so she decided to return to her natural weight. She put on 32 kg (70 pounds), and became the world's best known plus size model.

Major achievements: Crystal has been the face of high street clothing chains Mango and Evans, and has appeared in ad campaigns for H&M, Chanel and Dolce & Gabbana, and on the catwalk for Jean Paul Gaultier.

Secrets of success: Crystal is an inspiration to real women that beauty comes in all shapes and sizes.

Crystal is the only plus-size model to appear on the cover of 'Harper's Bazaar'.

Life Story

For years, Crystal Renn struggled to be something she wasn't. She would eat lettuce and chewing gum for lunch, and spend eight hours on the running machine in the gym. At the end of the day, she would be so tired, she could barely walk home. Then, despite all the diet and exercise, she started to put on weight!

Questions and Answers

Q Why did you want to become a model?

A 'Ninety-nine percent of girls want to be models because they think that they will wear expensive clothes, make loads of money and travel a lot. That never interested me. I wanted to make art, to create an image with a photographer. And I wanted to get out of [my home town] in Mississippi!'

Crystal Renn, *Der Spiegel* 2009

Q What changes would you make to the fashion industry?

A ' I don't want to see 14 girls all the same size on the runway. I want variety. Different sizes, skin colours, hair. Then there wouldn't be so much pressure on models to conform to one ideal. Models should just be beautiful women who inspire others.'

Crystal Renn, *Der Spiegel* 2009

That was the turning point the young model needed. She realised she could never be the size and shape of her fellow models. But maybe she could be successful in another way. She found a supportive model agency, started eating healthily again, and became the most famous plus size model in the world. 'Plus size' is the name given to models over a UK size 12.

At 23, Crystal wrote a book called *Hungry*, about her experiences in the fashion industry, which became a best seller. Her modelling career continues to go from strength to strength, and perhaps most positively she has started a trend for plus size models in the fashion industry. Crystal's story has inspired millions of young women.

Crystal at a book signing for her autobiography 'Hungry' in New York in 2009.

Andrej Pejic

THE TOP MAN IN WOMENSWEAR

With his bleached blonde hair and fine features, Andrej has found success modelling menswear and womenswear.

Stats!

Full name: Andrej Pejic

Date and place of birth: 28 August 1991 in Tuzla, Bosnia

Stats: Height 6ft 2in (1.88m), chest 36in (91cm), waist 30in (76cm)

First break: Andrej was born in Bosnia but moved to Australia at the age of eight with his family to escape the Bosnian war. At 16 he was working part-time in McDonald's in Melbourne when a model scout came in to order a hamburger. He told Andrej to come into the agency the next day, and signed him straight away.

Major achievements: Andrej has worked with famous photographers Steven Meisel, and Mert and Marcus for *Paris Vogue* and *Italian Vogue*. Jean Paul Gaultier has cast him in his men's and women's shows at Paris Fashion Week 2011. Marc Jacobs has used Andrej for his men's shows, and in the ad campaign for Marc by Marc Jacobs.

Secrets of success: Andrej has a unique ability to switch between menswear and womenswear – and make both look great!

When he retires from modelling, Andrej plans to go to university to study either law or economics.

Life Story

When Andrej Pejic met his first model agent, he wasn't sure if the agent realised he was a boy and not a girl. At the agency the next day, with any confusion cleared up, Andrej was told he was unlikely to break into menswear in Australia. Every country has its own distinctive fashion market, and Australian menswear was just too, well, manly for him.

Andrej models womenswear for French designer Jean Paul Gaultier during Paris Fashion Week in March 2011.

So Andrej borrowed some money from his mum and started travelling the world, from London to Paris to New York, picking up agencies along the way. In London, his agency Storm Models shows his pictures in the men's and the women's section of their website.

In Paris he quickly found regular work, but it was only when *Paris Vogue* dressed him in women's clothes for an editorial shoot that the fashion world really took notice. Now at fashion weeks from Paris to New York, Andrej strides down the catwalk for as many women's shows as he does men's. His look is unique, and Andrej turns heads and challenges prejudices wherever he goes.

Questions and Answers

Q Do you prefer modelling menswear or womenswear?

A 'I'm comfortable doing both. Although womenswear is more glamorous. The clothes are more exciting. In menswear I have to work more at having a masculine presence. But that's my job!'

Andrej Pejic , *The Telegraph* 2011

Q Were your school friends surprised to see you modelling womenswear?

A 'Well, since I've been a teenager, I've always been experimental. So they weren't surprised. But wearing a wedding dress for a [Jean Paul Gaultier] show was probably something they didn't expect! But they're all supportive.'

Andrej Pejic , *The Telegraph* 2011

Heidi Klum

Birthday: 1 June 1973

Home: Born in Bergisch Gladbach, Germany. Lives in New York City, USA

Stats: Height 5ft 9.25in (1.76m), dress size 6 UK

Fast fact: Estimated to be the second highest earning fashion model ever, behind Gisele

Background: A friend entered Heidi for a national modelling contest with a first prize of US$300,000 (£188,000), which she won! She put her education on hold and moved to New York to model full time.

Big break: In 1997 Heidi did her first catwalk show for lingerie brand Victoria's Secret and ended up working with them for 13 years! In 1998 she became the first German model to appear on the cover of *Sports Illustrated's* swimsuit edition.

Career highs: Following her success as a model, Heidi has moved into new areas. Since 2004, she has presented the US reality show 'Project Runway'. More recently she has launched a range of sportswear.

Website: www.heidiklum.com

Lara Stone

Birthday: 20 December 1983

Home: Born in Geldrop, Holland. Lives in London, UK.

Stats: Height 5ft 10in (1.78m), dress size 8 UK

Fast fact: Married to *Little Britain* comedian David Walliams

Background: Lara was discovered on the Paris Metro when she was 14. She was entered for the Elite Model Look competition the following year, and although she didn't win, the agency decided to sign her.

Big break: In 2006 Lara made her catwalk debut at Paris Fashion Week, and the fashion world started to take notice. She appeared on the cover of *Paris Vogue* and was included in 'Top Ten Models to Watch' by New York Magazine.

Career highs: In 2010 Calvin Klein signed Lara to be the face of not one, but three of their brands! The same year, she was voted Model of the Year at the British Fashion Awards.

Website: http://www.supermodels.nl/larastone

Agyness Deyn

Birthday: 16 February 1983

Home: Born in Oldham, Manchester UK. Lives in New York City, USA

Stats: Height 5ft 8in (1.73m), dress size 6 UK

Fast fact: Used to work in a fish and chip shop

Background: Born Laura Hollins, but changed her name after consulting a numerology expert (each letter is given a number value and the 'score' when they are added together gives a definition of what sort of person you are). Agyness was childhood friends with the fashion designer Henry Holland, and was spotted by a model scout while visiting Holland in London.

Big break: Agyness's career took off when she met influential UK fashion editor Katie Grand, who helped her find an agent in New York.

Career highs: Has modelled for Burberry, Armani, Paul Smith and Vivienne Westwood. The face of Jean Paul Gaultier fragrance Ma Dame. Named in the top 30 models of the decade by *Paris Vogue*. Voted Model of the Year 2007 at the British Fashion Awards.

Website: http://www.supermodels.nl/agynessdeyn

Mark Vanderloo

Birthday: 24 April 1968
Home: Born in Waddinxveen, Holland. Lives in New York City, USA

Stats: Height 6ft 2in (188cm), chest 40in (101cm), waist 32in (81cm)

Fast fact: The look of a character in the video game *Mass Effect* was modelled on Mark

Background: Mark was studying history at the University of Amsterdam when he went along to a photoshoot with his model girlfriend. The photographer needed a male model for a second shoot he was doing and Mark agreed to step in.

Big break: Mark's pictures landed on the desk of international agency Wilhelmina, and within months Mark was on catwalk at Paris, Milan and New York fashion weeks. Two years later he moved to New York, and was signed as the face of Calvin Klein's Obsession fragrance.

Career highs: Mark was voted VH1 Male Model of the Year in 1996. He has been the face of Hugo Boss since 2005

Website: http://models.com/models/Mark-Vanderloo

Sean O'Pry

Birthday: 5 July 1989

Home: Born in Kennesaw, Georgia, USA. Lives in New York City, USA

Stats: Height 6ft 1in (1.85m), chest 40in (101cm), waist 30in (76cm)

Fast fact: Sean has twice been bitten by a snake

Background: Sean was a normal high school student who enjoyed baseball and American football, and planned to study marine biology at university.

Big break: The 17-year-old was scouted from his prom photos on social networking site MySpace. At first he didn't believe he was being approached by a real model agency!

Career highs: Sean has consistently ranked in the top five male models in the world. He has starred in ad campaigns for Calvin Klein, Armani, Dolce & Gabanna, Marc Jacobs and others, and on the catwalk for Versace, YSL and Givenchy.

Website: http://nymag.com/fashion/models/sopry/seanopry/

Adriana Lima

Birthday: 12 June 1981

Home: Born in Salvador, Bahia, Brazil. Lives New York City, USA

Stats: Height 5ft 10in (1.78m), dress size 6 UK

Fast fact: Appeared in a 2008 episode of the US series *Ugly Betty*, playing herself

Background: Adriana was a regular in local model pageants at school. At 15, she entered – and won – the prestigious Ford 'Supermodel of Brazil' 1995 model search, and came second in the 'Supermodel of the World' contest the following year.

Big break: In 1999, Adriana did her first fashion show for lingerie company Victoria's Secret. She was offered a contract in 2000 and has been working with them ever since. She even appeared in a TV ad during the US Super Bowl that was watched by 103 million people!

Career highs: Adriana has worked for Guess?, cosmetics brand Maybelline and fashion labels Armani, Versace and Louis Vuitton.

Website: www.adrianalima.com

More fashion models to look out for

Candice Swanepoel – South Africa
Natalia Vodianova – Russia
Daria Werbowy – Ukraine
Bar Rafaeli – Israel
Allesandra Ambrosio – Brazil

Simon Nessman – Canada
Francisco Lachowski – Brazil
Luke Worrall – UK
David Agbodji – France
Yuri Pleskun – Russia

Index

Celebrity Secrets

Contents of the books in the series:

Extreme Sports People
9780750265669
Lewis Hamilton
Jordy Smith
Lynn Hill
Sébastien Foucan
Shanaze Reade
Danny Way
Shaun White
Ann Trason
Anne-Caroline Chausson
Other Extreme Sports People

Fashion Designers
9780750264693
Marc Jacobs
Jimmy Choo
Miuccia Prada
Tom Ford
Stella McCartney
Yohji Yamamoto
Paul Smith
Kate and Laura Mulleavy
Dolce and Gabbana
Other Fashion Designers

Film Stars
9780750264679
Zac Efron
Amanda Seyfried
Robert Pattinson
Carey Mulligan
Jake Gyllenhaal
Kristen Stewart
Johnny Depp
Zoe Saldana
Daniel Radcliffe
Other Film Stars

Footballers
9780750264686
Wayne Rooney
Cristiano Ronaldo
Steven Gerrard
David Villa
Carlos Tévez
Wesley Sneijder
David Beckham
Andrés Iniesta
Rio Ferdinand
Other Footballers

Pop Stars
9780750264273
Lady Gaga
Dizzee Rascal
Rihanna
Justin Bieber
Beyoncé
Jason Derülo
Pixie Lott
Jay-Z
Miley Cyrus
Other Pop Stars

TV Celebrities
9780750265652
Matt Smith
Tess Daly
Angela Griffin
Holly Willoughby
Dermot O'Leary
Harry Hill
Simon Cowell
Sarah Beaney
Cheryl Cole
Other TV Celebrities

Internet Sensations
9780750267779
Bip Ling
Ok Go
Shane Dawson
Dane Boedigheimer
Fred
Michelle Phan
Simon Totfield
Charlie McDonnell
Justin Bieber
Other Internet Sensations

Young Royals
9780750267724
Prince William
Prince Harry
Princesses Beatrice and Eugenie
Charlotte Casiraghi
Princess Sikhanyiso
Prince Azim
Princess Victoria
Princess Sirivannavari
Prince Carl Phillip of Sweden
Other Young Royals

World Sports Champions
9780750267731
Xavi Hernàndez
Usain Bolt
Jessica Ennis
Mao Asada
Sebastian Vettel
Oscar Pistorius
Tirunesh Dibaba
Victoria Pendleton
Rafael Nadal
Other World Sports Champions

Millionaires
9780750267748
Mark Zuckerberg
Jonathan Koon
Stacey Bendet
Jamie Murray Wells
Maddie Bradshaw
Andrew Mason
Michelle Mone
Farrah Gray
Oprah Winfrey
Other Millionaires

Fashion Models
9780750267755
Gisele Bündchen
Kate Moss
Lily Cole
Tyson Beckford
Baptiste Giabiconi
David Gandy
Tyra Banks
Crystal Renn
Andrej Pejic
Other Fashion Models

Reality TV Stars
9780750267762
Kim Kardashian
Ashley Banjo
JLS
Michael Sorrentino
Cher Lloyd
Paris Hilton
Peter Andre
Audrina Patridge
Jordin Sparks
Other Reality TV Stars

WAYLAND